From Hell to Jackson Hole

From Hell to Jackson Hole

A POETIC HISTORY OF THE AMERICAN WEST

by

Michael L. Johnson

Bridge House Books • Rancho Murieta, CA

Works of Art

Page 2:
Bill Reid, Haida
"The Raven and the First Men," 1980
Wood sculpture
Museum of Anthropology
Vancouver, Canada
Photo: Bill McLennan

Page 26:
Albert Bierstadt
"Emigrants Crossing the Plains," 1867
Oil on canvas
National Cowboy and Western
Heritage Museum
Oklahoma City, OK

Page 30:
Margaretta (Mrs. Jonas W.) Brown
"Hydraulic Mining in the Boise Basin
in the Early Seventies," c. 1870-1880
Oil on canvas
Idaho State Historical Society
Boise, ID

Page 64:
James Earle Fraser
"The End of the Trail," 1915
Plaster
National Cowboy and Western
Heritage Museum
Oklahoma City, OK

Page 70:
Charles M. Russell
"In without Knocking," 1909
Oil on canvas
Amon Carter Museum
Fort Worth, TX

Page 82:
Georgia O'Keeffe
"Deer's Skull with Pedernal," 1936
Oil on canvas
Boston Museum of Fine Arts
Boston, MA
Georgia O'Keeffe Foundation
Artists Rights Society
New York, NY

Page 90:
Peter Hurd
"The Gate and Beyond," 1952
Egg tempera on panel
Roswell Museum and Art Center
Roswell, NM
Gift of the artist

Page 122:
Edd Hayes
"The Champ," 1988
Bronze, larger than life-size
ProRodeo Hall of Fame and Museum
of the American Cowboy
Colorado Springs, CO

Copyright © 2001 by Michael L. Johnson

Library of Congress Catalog Card No. 2001 131220
ISBN 0-9653487-7-6

Interior design by Pete Masterson, Aeonix Publishing Group, www.aeonix.com
Cover design by Allen Takeshita, Neo Design, www.neodesign.com
Cover photo by Christine M. Miller, MilChristine@aol.com

Published by
Bridge House Books
P.O. Box 809
Rancho Murieta, CA 95683
www.bridgehousebooks.com

Printed by C&C Offset Printing Company, Ltd. in China.

No place, not even a wild place, is a place until it has had that human attention that at its highest reach we call poetry.

Wallace Stegner, "The Sense of Place"

Geography did not determine the boundaries of the West; rather, history created them. The West that Americans recognize in the twentieth century is their own work.

Richard White, *"It's Your Misfortune and None of My Own": A New History of the American West*

History is the essence of innumerable biographies.

Thomas Carlyle, *On History*

Contents

From Hell to Jackson Hole

Foreword: Cowboy Poem

This poem rises before dawn,;
guzzles strong coffee; gobbles eggs
over easy with bacon, grits,
biscuits, and red-eye gravy; then
begins its day of lonely work:
riding the line on the mind's ranch,
keeping the words under its charge
on home range, pulling them from bogs,
tending to their various ills,
protecting them from predators.

This poem in the saddle goes
dashing, rolls its own smokes, sometimes
may need to take its guns to town.

This poem has an evening sip
of whiskey, ponders the long view,
sleeps in a shack under clear stars.

This poem has a quick and wry
sense of humor, gets the job done,
dallies its rope, dallies its tongue.

Acknowledgments

I'm grateful to the Hall Center for the Humanities at the University of Kansas for the Creative Work Fellowship that granted me the time and research funding to undertake and complete the writing of this book. Many thanks to the capable staff of the College Word Processing Center at KU for patiently translating all my scribbling, through several drafts, into immaculate final copy. Special thanks to Naida West, who believed in this project from the start and took it to the finish in style.

Some of the poems herein first appeared in the following publications: *The Acorn: A Journal of the Western Sierra, Aethlon: The Journal of Sport Literature, Amaranth, Architrave, Bogg, Brown Dog Review, The Cape Rock, The Cathartic, Coal City Review, Crab Creek Review, Ecphrases: Poems as Interpretations of the Other Arts* (Topeka, Kansas: Woodley Press, 1989), *Ekphrasis: A Poetry Journal, Familiar Stranger* (Lawrence, Kansas: Flowerpot Mountain Press, 1983), *Hellas, Heritage of the Great Plains, Hodge Podge Poetry, Midwest Quarterly, Nerve Cowboy, The New York Street Reading Series Anthology: Poetry and Prose by Guests of the New York Street Reading Series in Lawrence, Kansas, 1996-97* (Kansas City, Missouri: NYS Press, 1997), *Owen Wister Review, Parting Gifts, Piedmont Literary Review, Plainsongs, Salt Fork Review, Slant: A Journal of Poetry, The Snail's Pace Review, The Unicorn Captured* (Lawrence, Kansas: Cottonwood Review Press, 1980), *XY Files: Poems on the Male Experience* (Santa Fe, New Mexico: Sherman Asher Publishing, 1997). A much longer, prose version of "The Johnson County War, 1892" appeared in the *Journal of Unconventional History* as "The Interpretations of the Other Arts" and Johnson County Variations."

Frijoles Canyon

Touch this soft tuff,
and know one thing
the wind has loved
longer than skin.

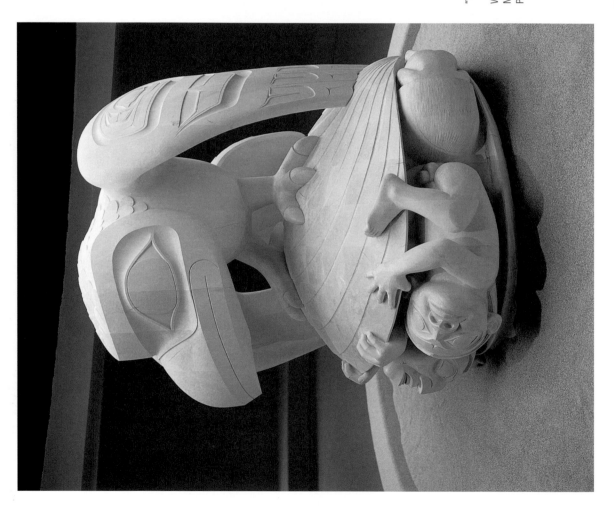

"The Raven and the First Men,"
by Bill Reid, Haida, 1980
Wood sculpture, 210 cm high
Museum of Anthropology, Vancouver, Canada
Photo: Bill McLennan

Bill Reid, *The Raven and the First Men*

Raven on this day might have been
creating the world, flinging stars
and sun and moon into the sky,
stocking rivers and sea with fish,
or changing to another form.

Instead, cedar-carved, he declares
a moment of ancestral past
here forever where he has found
the first men, embryonic, dazed,
cowering in a clam shell while
he, perched atop it, coaxes them
to venture out onto the sand

and you to leave your self and hold
all spirit wings unfold above.

Entradas

Sure as shipwreck had left them on the coast
of what's now Texas, Cabeza de Vaca and his
  companions were lost,
those would-be slavers soon enslaved
by Indians—though they managed to get free.

Eight years later those Spaniards headed west,
then south, through unmapped land,
greeted along the way by tribe on tribe
as peaceful healers, shamans, prophets, and
  merchants between
two worlds. Trading on otherness, they changed,
enough to be appalled:
their fellow Christians had destroyed so much,
making chattels of everyone they hadn't killed.

When Cabeza de Vaca and his naked native retinue
stumbled into New Spain,
things got culturally complex, and, worse,
the drifters told stories of cities to the north
replete with gold.

Fray Marcos traveled, reconnoitered, and returned
with utopian lies.

Coronado listened and spun
imperial fancies of Cíbola;
but when, after hard months horseback,
he and his young adventurers approached
some pueblo's mud-brick walls, he knew he'd found
nothing magnificent at all.
The skin beneath his gilded armor itched
in the summer heat. On the sun-fired ground
Zuñi warriors drew lines
with sacred cornmeal, which they warned
the Spaniards not to cross.

José de Gálvez, 1729-1787

Travel across the difficult gulf
fraught with peril, an all-land route
to Baja California the first imperative
of colonization, this aspiring man,
special emissary of Carlos III, turned
his energies to solutions. He took charge
of the precarious campaign against
the Seri and Pima rebels. He sought
peace in Sonora. But his mind
slipped. At Pitic he emerged
from his tent late one night and told
some perplexed officer his plan to dress
six hundred Guatamalan monkeys like
soldiers and send them forth to storm
Cerro Prieto, the Indian stronghold.
In the months ahead he believed he was
various great personages, at last
God Almighty. He got better but then,
like the viceroyalty itself, went down before
Thomas Jefferson's expanding dream
as the American epic began.

Sacagawea

Wintering with the Mandans,
Lewis and Clark engaged
Toussaint Charbonneau,
trapper, cook, interpreter,
and otherwise a man
as useless in a boat
as teats on a boar.

The bonus was his young
Shoshone wife, whose mere
presence would prove the corps
came in peace, who didn't
so much guide America
westward as keep it
from losing its way
in distances that struck
those white men dumb.

Wild West Haiku No. 1

Zebulon Pike halts
the expedition: a peak
reaching to heaven.

John Colter

Finished serving Lewis and Clark, he soon
departed for the territory, wound
back to the northern Rockies. He stayed west
another five years. He trapped fur and fought
with Flatheads 'gainst the Blackfeet; and one time
the Blackfeet caught him, stripped him, made him run
so they could hunt him down, but he escaped
and walked by night over two hundred miles
from Three Forks, Montana, to Lisa's fort.

Alone: way of the first white man to see
and circumnavigate the Teton Range.

Before his short life ended in a bed—
later, in Missouri—he carved his name
on trees and rocks from hell to Jackson Hole,
the boundless bowl of sky above.
                                        We know

no oracle that drove such wandering:
only a man off in a virgin world
he dreamed he had completely to himself,
at last elusive as the tales he told.

Meriwether Lewis

... the thick applause that welcomed his journey
swelled and tapered like a slow exhale.

Linda Bierds, "Light, Steam"

Sunset. The governor arrives at Grinder's Stand.
He rides in from the south on the old Natchez Trace
after fording the Tennessee and Buffalo.
Behind him ride his servant and John Neelly's slave,
the first leading a packhorse bearing massive trunks.
In front: two mud-chinked cabins. Around: wilderness.

Grinder's wife greets the party, and Lewis requests
lodging. Neelly, hunting for strayed horses, should soon
catch up. Lewis gets a cabin. Servant and slave,
sent to the barn, stay there. The great explorer eats
little before he retires to his bearskin bed,
Mississippi-to-Pacific trip for some time
blurred, afloat. In self-doubt, opiates, alcohol.

Thirty years later Grinder's wife still tells the rest
in countless versions. Alone and delirious,
sleepless, Lewis paces back and forth on the path
between the cabins. Babbling. Then three men ride in,
wanting somewhere to sleep. He threatens with a brace
of pistols. They ride off. Later she hears gunfire.
Lewis at her door begging water for his wounds.

She's terrified, keeps him shut out. She waits. A gourd
scraping the side of the water bucket. She sends
her children out to the barn to wake the men there.
They find Lewis in his cabin. Part of his head
blown away. A hole in his chest. He never gains
consciousness and dies before dawn. Or he crawls off
into the dark and gets carried back. Or he kills
himself with a razor. Or—what? But hastily
he's buried some distance north of the cabins. Oak
coffin. Maybe an inquest. Maybe not. His grave
unmarked till mid-century. Murder? Suicide?

Suspects: several, unproven. Jefferson, like
Clark, who later changes his mind, thinks suicide.
Many don't agree. But something went wrong for this
moody young man unfit for political life.

Neelly forwards to Jefferson all that is left
of Lewis—trunks, rifle, watch, flintlock pistols, dirk—
the hundred dollars on his person never found.

The Lourdes of America

After Fray Sebastian Alvarez had checked out
the stories of a light
on a hill near the Santa Cruz
and of a mobile crucifix,
he wrote a letter to the Episcopal See
in Durango. He mentioned no specific fact,
but there was something there.

Pilgrims in droves
came to the Santuario de Chimayó.
They still do. Three hundred thousand a year.

Through a low door just to the left
of the altar, you find two sacristies.
One is cluttered with *bultos*, crutches, images of Christ.
The other, smaller, has a hole
in the floor that never runs out
of the dry earth people carry away
in compacts, envelopes, and soft-drink cups:
a slight geography of hope.

The Santa Fe Trail

When William Becknell first packed into Santa Fe, hogbacks'
jumbled rocks red as Christ's blood behind, he couldn't foretell
all the profit he would make from his modest enterprise.
Or all the caravans to follow, greedy men camped south
of town before the last leg in, bright visions of sweet cakes,
tequila, fiestas, reckless gambling, flirtatious whores
dancing in their heads. Treaties. Forts and sutlers' stores strewn out
along the long miles from Missouri. Indian attacks.
Civil War battles. Homesteaders. Murders. Holdups. Rails webbed
across the High Plains. Endless massacres of buffalo.
Artists. Tourists. Postcards. Four-lane highways. Historical
markers. Museums. Urban refugees. Enduring ruts.

Wild West Haiku No. 2

Searching for water,
doomed Jedediah Smith finds
Comanches as well.

Sir William Drummond Stewart, 1833

Why'd he come from Scotland to hunt the Western wild?
Because he'd quarreled with his brother John,
Lord of Grandtully and of Murthley Castle.
Also because he wanted to avoid the hassle
of marriage ruefully attendant on
his having gotten some trim-ankled servant girl with child.

Prior to Heading Downriver and Back to Civilization, German Prince Alexander Maximilian, Having by Early 1834 Witnessed Enough of the Exotic Northern West, Writes of His Disgust at Life among the Traders at Fort Clark

The Mandans and Hidatsas fascinate
still, and Bodmer has done most splendid work
in rendering the romance of their world;
but a long winter spent in our so-called
cabin out on a bleak peninsula
in an ice-locked river, its leaky walls
lashed by the relentless Dakota wind,
has tried us hard. We have grown tired of this
ramshackle hole to the highest degree.
Daily routine is conducted in such
a filthy manner that it nauseates.
Our Negro cook suffers from a severe
rheumatic disease, so we have seen fit
to hire another, named Boileau. The best
we could come by, he handles cups and plates
with fingers much used for cleaning his nose
as peasants do. Kipp, the clerk of the fort,
has habits scarcely better, and his boy
wears trousers with a gap both front and back
in order that he may relieve himself
casually and quickly on the floor,
which happens all too often during meals.
We are, be assured, anxious to depart.

Nancy Kelsey, 1841

Far, far
from Sapling Grove
and easy hope of easy wagoning,
the party took a southwest fork
somewhere west of the Rockies, and the going grew
arduous, lots of spots so steep
she had to carry her one-year-old in her arms.

The desiccated flats
glimmered with heat and salt
and stretched off into grassless vacancy.

She ate ox, climbed barefoot across
the Sierra Nevada, and near her wits' end
made it to the San Joaquin.

                    The next year,
John Marsh's booster lies about the route
forgotten, other intrepid souls came,
more the year after that,
then more and more
and more. . . .

An American Story

John C. Frémont was an ambitious man.
So, forsaking Georgia, he headed out,
plumbed wilderness as if it were his own
front yard, wrote it down for people back east.
He made Kit Carson famous as a scout
but left him behind once and got his crew
snowbound in the Rockies while searching for
a way to put rails through—they ate their shoes,
then comrades. He led California's fight
against Mexico, ran for President,
commanded the West in the Civil War,
invested badly, became governor
of Arizona Territory, died
tombstone-broke in a New York boardinghouse.

Oregon Territory

After Jefferson cut his deal, opponents jeered.
What does he want that worthless desert for?
What's on the other side?'
Fur and more fur.

Later, eager to win Indian souls
for Presbyterians' conceit of God,
deluded Marcus and Narcissa Whitman took
their honeymoon on the Oregon Trail.
Along the way, she got with child
while broken-down wagons got left behind
and trappers and traders they traveled with
got weary of the sermons and delays.

The Whitmans went to work on Cayuse land,
land Marcus claimed was undeserved
by heathens who refused conversion. Time
tempered large hopes with orphans, labor, solitude.

Measles and confused millennial beliefs drove
the Cayuse to rebel and kill
the Whitmans and a dozen fellow dupes.

But soon there came enough
soldiers, railroaders, dam-builders, and lumberjacks
to make the place nigh safe
for plaid-clad yuppies, pseudo-Native spiritualists,
and latte-sipping hippies and their ilk.

Brigham Young

Tired, Brigham Young died
1877
but lived to live out
his visions: led five thousand
Mormons, all obsessed
by angelic messages
engraved on gold plates
Joseph Smith purportedly
found in a stone box,
out of Illinois; pushed on
westward to a bleak
paradise in the desert
of his Deseret;
fathered Salt Lake City and,
though a moralist
who didn't revel in sex,
fifty-six kids by
sixteen holy vessels. He
hailed from Whitingham,
Vermont, where, at his birthplace,
now a patch of weeds
ending a well-furrowed road,
there's a plain marker:
BRIGHAM YOUNG BORN ON THIS SPOT
1801
A MAN OF MUCH COURAGE AND
SUPERB EQUIPMENT

Samuel Chamberlain Recalls "Judge" Holden

An army private turned deserter in the war
with Mexico, I met the judge in forty-nine.
I'd joined Captain Glanton's gang of scalp-hunters hired
by Chihuahua to stop Comanche plundering.
He was second in command. *Who* he was none knew,
although a more stonehearted villain never went
unhanged. He stood six feet in moccasins, his frame
large and fleshy, his face tallow-colored and dull,
devoid of hair and all expression. His desires
were blood and women. In the camp I heard grim tales
of horrid crimes he'd perpetrated when he bore
another name in Texas or the Cherokee
Nation. And before we left Fronteras, a girl
only ten years old was found in the chaparral,
her body foully violated, with the mark
of a huge hand on her small throat. Beyond a doubt
he was the culprit, but he wasn't ever charged.
Yet once I saw him seize the captain while the man
sprayed oaths and bullets during one of his tirades
and lay him down and soothe him into drunken sleep.
Moreover, he was current in the sciences
and fluent in a dozen tongues. He played guitar
and harp at many a fandango, could out-waltz
any *poblana* of the ball, rode well, and shot
plumb center with rifle or revolver. Withal
an arrant coward whom I hated at first sight.

Argonauts

Greedy and bold, by dreams beguiled,
they lit out for the wild.
In letters home they told
of gain and loss—
but most, in time, much less of gold
and a deal more of dross.

Joaquin Murieta

For Naida West

Robin Hood of El Dorado or not,
out in that borderland of civilized
and savage, he was, for some, just one man;
for others, many—either way, at war
with wrong or right. For some, he never did
exist; for others, he lived on, at peace
after brief banditry, till he died old.
For some, prized angel; for others, feared beast.

For some, he ended as a severed head
pickled in booze, a grisly spectacle
of finitude that toured the mining towns;
for others, he remains, his story told
and told again, the spirit, glorious
on horseback still (but still a good bit short
of Zorro), sort of defending and sort
of avenging the past and its oppressed.

Adah Isaacs Menken

Toast of San Francisco, she wowed the West
playing Mazeppa, the Cossack prince lashed
birthday naked to a wild stallion's back
in punishment for some illicit love.
She filled the stage with frenzies of the flesh.

Many men damned her; most fell at her feet
and gave her gold or shares of mining stock.

Once, in Virginia City, Mark Twain came
to call at her hotel. She sipped champagne
and fed her lap dog brandied sugar cubes.
He spoke in riddles of her pretty hands.

Sand Creek

After all that happened before
the murder of Lean Bear,
after Black Kettle sent
a letter seeking peace,
after he and the other chiefs
wagoned to Denver to negotiate,
after their people came
to Fort Lyon, after Wynkoop told them to camp
at Sand Creek, after the men left to hunt,
after Chivington set up cannon on high ground
one cold morning between first light
and sunrise and drove his drunken troops down
on the village, after the official report

turned out to be less than complete,
after the public was appalled,
after the Cheyenne runners carried war pipes
        everywhere,
after Black Kettle still forgave,
after the tribes had nothing left to lose,
after blood rivered the central Great Plains,
after all that has happened since,
after all that will happen yet,
let this image suffice:
a soldier riding forth once more,
a woman's genitals
stretched on his saddlebow.

Davis K. Tutt

Unable to resolve a debt
dispute, he and Bill Hickok met
one evening on a Springfield street
and stood apart two hundred feet.
Both drew and fired. His shot missed. But
Wild Bill's did not—the last of Tutt.

That was our dream incarnadined,
the first fast-gun fight of its kind.

Wild West Haiku No. 3

A farmer's daughter
meets Cole Younger and begins
to become Belle Starr.

Albert Bierstadt, "Emigrants Crossing the Plains," 1867   Oil on canvas, 60" x 96"   (72.19C.13) National Cowboy and Western Heritage Museum, Oklahoma City, OK

Albert Bierstadt, *Emigrants Crossing the Plains* (1867)

Golden, sublime,
those spokes of light
in warm barrage
that, dimming, climb
cliffs to the right
will prove in time
truth or mirage.

John Wesley Hardin

Texas' most notorious killer and no doubt
a homicidal maniac, he bragged about
his many notches, their tales later told
in his own hand, each justified without
remorse. But for an instant wear
the boots of a fifteen-year-old
student of death, maybe victim of violent
circumstances, mercurial and ill at ease,
just before he will take
his first life: you don't scare
at the black man intent
on beating you; with abstract care
you draw the Colt won in a poker game
and hold it like a rattlesnake
whose long bite you can aim
at anyone you please.

Anna Judah

Mocked by many, Theodore Judah lived
only to dream a railroad reaching all the way
across the country, but he died
of yellow fever caught in Panama
six years before the spikes
were driven, an event none thought
to ask his widow to attend.

Ever his advocate, forgotten and alone
back in her Massachusetts home—
that very day their anniversary—
she sought a deeper happiness and felt
the soul of her obsessed husband descend
on her, and so together they were there
at Promontory Point.

Margaretta (Mrs. Jonas W.) Brown, "Hydraulic Mining in the Boise Basin in the Early Seventies," painted circa 1870–1880

Oil on canvas, 26½" x 20¾"
Idaho State Historical Society Collection, Boise, ID

Mrs. Jonas W. Brown, *Hydraulic Mining in the Boise Basin in the Early Seventies* (circa 1870-80)

Hierarchy of a battle. Below,
in the canyon, men in identical
pale slickers cannon water that could tear
down a fortress against the yielding slope,
flushing a mountain of gold-laden dirt
into gullies. Up above, on the ridge,
before a backdrop of soft, rounded peaks
half cleared of timber, men in suits look on,
the women with them finding in all this
rapine something of interest, perhaps.

Wild West Haiku No. 4

Wife split, fortune blown,
dreamy Henry Comstock drifts
north, then shoots himself.

Luna Warner

One Kansas day
back in the seventies
it snowed from dawn to dusk,

and the wind blew so hard
we couldn't even see
the Solomon.

Our chickens all
were stuck against
the woodpile, frozen stiff.

Wild West Haiku No. 5

At Hyer's cobblershop
a drover shares his concept:
pointed toes, slant heels.

John Simpson Chisum

He built a cattle empire on free grass
and credit, but at last he lost his ass.

Deconstructing Custer

A tall six feet—so claimed his wife.
And thus did adoration mess
with truth to glorify fey life.

The records at West Point disclose
what eager heroizing chose
to slight: he stood some inches less.

Wild West Haiku No. 6

His back to a door,
oddly, Wild Bill Hickok checks
his hand: aces, eights.

A Homicide in the Old West

One ordinary August afternoon
of poker at a nondescript saloon
in Deadwood, South Dakota, Jack McCall
shot Wild Bill Hickok in the head. The ball
passed through and lodged in William Massie's wrist.

The victim sat still and then, with a twist
aside, slumped to the floor. His body bled
out quickly, and thereafter Doc Pierce said
his long, tapering fingers looked like marble.
Most of the rest is legendary garble.

Wild West Haiku No. 7

Hungry, the Sioux chiefs
sign a treaty: the Black Hills
for government food.

Quanah Parker

After he lost
the Llano Estacado, this
fearless Comanche chief surrendered but

soon beat the whites
at their own game:
went on

to deal in cattle, bought
a house large enough to hold all
his wives, and painted stars

across the roof
so he'd outrank
any general who might happen by.

Renowned Harvard Botanist Asa Gray
and His Retinue Visit Colorado in 1877

A group photograph. Backdrop: a large tent
under ponderosas. Gray (lower left)
sits on the ground, legs folded, a plant press
across his lap. A buckskinned guide (far left)
and a black man holding a coffee pot
(far right), neither really a part of this
display, stand outside the circle of prim
persons clustered around a table spread
with linen in the picture's center, posed
agaze in various directions, swells
sporting a motley of hats, all of them,
save Gray's wife, looking scientifically
formal and self-important in their suits,
as comfortable in the wilderness
as absentminded Thomas Nuttall was
once, up on the Missouri, when he used
his gun to dig specimens from the shore
and got the barrel clogged with rocks and mud
and almost blew his genius to bits
when six hundred Sioux suddenly appeared.

T. A. McNeal, Soon to Be Editor of the Medicine
Lodge *Cresset*, Recounts His Entry into Journalism

When I entered the *Cresset* office
on that windy March day, there
sat Ezra Iliff at a pine table.
In front of him lay his Colt
revolver, fully loaded. His hair,
black and coarse as an Indian's, fell
down over his collar. His eyes,
dark and flashing, looked out
from under beetling brows
with hairs stiff and wiry and as long
as those of a mustache.
His dress was in keeping
with his appearance. Around his neck
was a red bandanna. His gray
woolen shirt, flowing open
at the throat, revealed in part

the muscular neck and hirsute chest.
He wore the leather chaps
common to the cowmen of the day,
and his pants, stuffed in his boots,
were held in place by a belt
well filled with loaded cartridges.
A woven rawhide quirt hung
from his left wrist. The heels
of his boots were ornamented
with savage-looking spurs.
He was ready to ride.
But he was not just then
thinking of the range. He was
engaged, as I recall, in writing
a most vigorous editorial.

Wild West Haiku No. 8

Thoughtfully hidden
in the outhouse: a pistol
for Billy the Kid.

Josephine Marcus

When the legend becomes fact, print the legend.

*A journalist in John Ford's The Man
Who Shot Liberty Valance*

The infamous nude photograph
supposedly taken around
the time she took Tombstone at age
eighteen is not of her, contend
astute historians. But why
does legend have it otherwise?
Maybe seeing her this way helps
explain why Sheriff Behan, thought
trothed to her, wanted Wyatt Earp,
who'd stolen her away, undone:

a veillike shawl slit up the front
reveals brave nipples and plump breasts;
a hood of long dark hair shades eyes
like sweet secrets floating above
the slightest pout of a soft mouth,
chin held high with theatric pride;
the exposed throat requests a kiss.

Rustling, insults, and politics
aside, was some such face what launched
the feud that left that famed corral
strewn with the wounded and the dead?

Jesse James

Later, haunted Bob Ford long dead in Creede,
his namesake son will practice law
and advise Henry King
concerning Paramount's account
of this man with crime in his bones.

But now, unarmed,
dusting a picture frame, he hears
a pistol cock,
and his head starts
to turn. A single shot,
and all that wrung insomniac attention drops
into itself
to hold
momently one
memoried thought:
his too-missed preacher father doomed
to gold-rush missionary dreams and cholera.

Red, shattered skull
cradled in Zee's lap, he chokes out
a lag word, half formed, maybe "God,"
prayer or curse.

Frank James

Jesse slain by a slug
from the rear, Youngers jailed
at last, his life become
drear fear, he got himself
off—even after he'd
ridden with Quantrill's goons
and killed with Bloody Bill—
and opened up his house
to tourists, took them through
for half a dollar, then
died at seventy-two,
content as any man.

Wilde West

Persuaded to expand his tour, Oscar Wilde wends
to Omaha and further west. Though the Great Plains
are redolent of blotting paper, he is moved
by crowds that flatter him with imitation: hands
hold lilies in hellos, and sunflowers decorate
lapels. Californians gawk at his Custer locks.
He likes the cloaks and broad-brimmed hats that miners wear;
adds them to his wardrobe, along with corduroys
and cowboy neckerchiefs; tucks his pants in his boots.
Many men make fun of him; but when he leaves, wives,
lovesick maidens, read his pirated poetry,
repaint walls and ceilings, throw out cut glass, exchange
chandeliers for brackets and rugs for tile, and yearn
for Queen Anne furniture in parlors somewhere else.

Chung Sun

We know the story: his tea-farm
figment of Gold Mountain success;
his being beaten, robbed, reduced
to digging ditches, then to forced
joblessness; and his long sail home.
But there's no photograph of him.
He alone saved his face.

The Saga of Elfego Baca as Related
by the Last Known Witness
of the Frisco Standoff

Juanita Baca gave birth to her son
right at the moment when she jumped to catch
a fly in a sort of softball-type game
called Las Iglesias—so they say—here
in Socorro, winter of sixty-five,
long before New Mexico was a state.

A year later, the Bacas pulled out for
Topeka, Kansas, everything they owned
packed in a wagon.

       While they camped one night
up around Estancia, Navajos
kidnapped Elfego; but they brought him back
after four days.

       That tell you anything?

The Bacas stayed in Topeka five years—
till half the family dropped from one mishap
or another. Those who were still alive
returned to Socorro. Elfego worked
on ranches in the area. He met
Billy the Kid on one of them. The two
became close friends. That's what Elfego said,

but he told a bunch of tales I suspect
are false; and he admired Billy the Kid
excessively. That was in eighty-one.

Three years later something occurred that cinched
Elfego's fame. And I swear it's all true.

At that point Elfego served as a clerk
for some Socorro merchant. Word arrived
that Frisco, near the Arizona line,
was under siege by John B. Slaughter's men,
drunk punchers from his huge spread on the loose,
trigger-happies rampaging through the streets.
Those ruthless bullies had lopped the balls off
a sheepherder. Took him to a saloon
and did it on the bar. And they'd tied up
one of the townies and shot him four times
after he'd protested their rowdiness.
Used him as a target while they bet drinks.

No local peace officer had the guts
to calm things down, so young Elfego swiped
a deputy sheriff's badge and took off

to tackle the job.

He rode to a place
stricken with terror, the deep sky itself
fissured, like cracked blue adobe, with fear.

He arrested the first son of a bitch
who fired a pistol in his presence. When
confronted by a dozen of the man's
compatriots demanding his release,
Elfego drew and fired and hit the mount
that Slaughter's ramrod sat. The critter flipped
over and crushed its rider on the spot.

Elfego brought his prisoner to court
the following day. He was fined a few
dollars. Of course, the matter didn't stop
at that, for scores of men from Slaughter's ranch
had barreled into town to seek revenge.

Women and children hidden in the church,
Elfego got off a shot or so, then
ran through lead thick as hail into a slant
jacal, its packed dirt floor well below ground
level. The frightened owner made a quick
farewell by the back door. The stage was set.

The cowboys surrounded Elfego's fort.
One rushed the building and fell in his tracks.
The rest opened up. Most emptied their guns
for thirty-odd hours. Even dynamite
had no effect. Once the dust from the blast
settled, smoke rose from the chimney of what
structure still stood. Smell of coffee and stew:
Elfego was fixing breakfast inside
the rubble.

But soon a real deputy
came from Socorro.

Slaughter's men withdrew,
dead and wounded in tow.

Elfego sprang
out through a window, six-gun in each hand.

Thousands of bullet holes riddled the house
he left behind.

He spent four months in jail.
Tried for murder, he was judged innocent.

Declared a hero by the Spanish folk,
he launched his legal and political
career in Socorro and well beyond.

He got involved with Pancho Villa, then
with President Huerta, and then with some
beautiful Mexican adventuress.
He survived automobile accidents.
Criminals surrendered to him by mail.
Would-be assassins failed and failed again.

Elfego's life was charmed. But die he would—
in Albuquerque at the tender age
of eighty. His span stretched from the Old West
till past the time when scientists dreamed dread
on horses through the hills near Trinity.
The bomb went off a month before his death.

Judge Roy Bean

Of law he held
differing views,
but in the Wild
West that's no news.

Mysterious Dave

He claimed direct descent from Cotton Mather,
though he never hunted witches
back home in Connecticut. Rather,
he ventured to the Southwest, there to kill
hombres who were pretty much sons of bitches.
And when the end of his criminal
career inexorably neared,
he jumped bail
and slowly disappeared.

Stages

1

The parlous and much-storied ride
on mountain steeps to Placerville
Hank Monk gave Horace Greeley just
to get him to a speech on time—
keep to schedule, above all else—
probably never did occur,
and yet its like is not unknown.

2

Uncle Jim Miller, Curly Dan,
Old Shalcross, and Dutch John drive
on.
Lonesome up front, butts bone-sore,
backs
locked in stiff curves, fingers gone
numb
from gripping the reins, they drive on.

3

Bored as the ash, poplar, and oak
that constitute the Concord coach,
lots of drivers carry a flask.

4

A driver questioned about what
he does for casualties in case
there's a bad accident responds,
"Them as is dead I let alone.
Them as is maimed I finish off
with the kingbolt. Dead folks don't
sue."

5

When Charlie Parkhurst, a man
known
for pushing his team hard, expires
in seventy-nine, he turns out
to be a woman in disguise.

6

Arctic winter of eighty-six,
a stage rolls into Camp Supply,
horses iced from muzzle to tail,
driver froze to death, passengers
huddled inside oblivious.

7

Dwarfed beneath high mesas and
buttes,
a disparate, desperate ship
of fools still rumbles through the dust
to Lordsburg in our John Ford dream,
everything always on the line.

Clay Allison, the Wild Wolf of the Washita

Sober, he was a model citizen;
but when he drank, he lost it all,
got paroxysmal, mean.

He sent a lot of men to hell,
then fell, insensible as stone,
beneath a wagon wheel.

Doc Holliday

The odds did not
stack up:
though he was whip-
crack fast,
he wasn't fast
enough to outdraw bad
tuberculosis.

When the house had
won all his money,
this gun who'd shot
so many
said only, in his last
moment of gambler gnosis,
"That's funny."

And passed.

A Bison Bull's Eye

Deep but blank: there's nothing behind
that onyx gape that could have guessed
how man would make, killing his kind,
an immense Treblinka of the West.

Failed Plains Homesteaders

Headed back east,
they said they just
flat couldn't stand
any more wind.

William H. Jackson Perched on Glacier Point, Composing a Panorama of the Yosemite Valley (circa 1888)

An unidentified photographer has caught him
where he always was: at the fulcrum
from which to turn his artifice
on fact and show a garden in the desert or
how pure nature is simply there
and can cradle railroads and offer wilderness
free of fear to folks in the East—
the West as fertile, healing, empty, vast.

The Johnson County War, 1892

In wooly Wyoming, cow-world tensions run high,
what with big companies stringing barbwire
and rustlers pilfering their calves. At last
the plutocrats get pissed off enough to declare
open season on maverickers or anyone else
(by and large, small ranchers and Democrats)
they want to see in hell.

After six men hang Cattle Kate in eighty-nine,
things get more edgy, rancorous.
The boom has ceased, and the smokers of big cigars
and drinkers of expensive bourbon spend
endless long months at the Cheyenne Club pondering
losses from droughts and blizzards, higher railroad rates,
falling beef demand, cowboys gone on strike,
overstocked ranges, pesky creditors,
stupid judgments, conflicts over water and grass,
the possible or imminent decline
of their own lifestyle. Something needs
to be done. A lot of that stuff
can't be fixed. And yet . . . what about a good
old-fashioned lynching bee?

Frank Canton and his cronies go
to Denver, gather a mishmash of killers (by and large,
Texans) and regulators, and bring them by train
back to Cheyenne. A list of names in hand,
they travel further north to Casper, blinds
drawn in the parlor car. Just outside town,
they disembark, unload their horses and supplies,
ready themselves to ride.

Major Frank Wolcott takes command.
The righteous army quickly leaves
the Casper rail yard and proceeds
wide of the sleeping town, the only sounds
the squeak of leather, grind and creak
of wagons, clink of metal gear.
Riding along, Wolcott reviews
the preparations: spy reports,
ample ammunition, telegraph lines
clipped to seal off the county—all of those particulars
that foretell certain victory.
We'll get rid of this trash, he vows,
the same way we got rid
of Indians.

They stop for breakfast, then ride on,
bound for Buffalo, where they mean
to seize the courthouse and disarm
the citizens. En route, however, Wolcott entertains
rumors of rustlers at the KC Ranch.
The army bivouacs. Alone in the dark,
he plots anew.

Morning's curve of sunlight descending from the Big-
          horns' peaks
and into their eastern foothills above
the Middle Fork of the Powder, trapper Bill Jones
exits the rickety cabin at the KC
to fetch some water. As he nears the stream,
its gurgling, clear in the cool air,
grows louder. But he hears
something different. Suddenly he's grabbed,
hustled away, and questioned. Who's inside?
How well armed? His partner, William Walker, comes out,
looks around, and soon also is in custody.
Neither is on the list. Others who are have left,
except for two.

When Nick Ray steps outside the cabin to investigate
the goings-on, bullets rip his body, staccato shots
echoing distantly in his brain as he crawls
toward the door. Nate Champion rushes forth,
half lifts and half drags him across
the threshold, shuts and bars the door, and tries,
to no avail, to keep his bleeding friend alive.
True to his name, he puts up a fight, suffers wounds,
even keeps a journal. Late in the afternoon,
Wolcott's men heap a wagon with hay and pitch pine,
torch it, and roll the blazing mess
against the cabin, which easily catches fire.
Champion dashes for a ravine,
doesn't make it, but has bought time
to let the county form
its counterforce.

That night, when Sheriff Red Angus and his posse arrive
at the KC, all that remains
is two bodies, ashes, charred wood.
Couriers scurry everywhere. Telegraph lines
hum again. Wolcott's half-ass militia has moved
up to the TA Ranch on Crazy Woman Creek
and taken refuge. More men join
the posse, and pickets are posted there.
At dawn the TA's buildings bristle with blue steel.
Battle begins.

A couple of days later, Wolcott's well-fortified guns,
low on everything, driven to extremes,
are binding dynamite in bundles when three troops
of cavalry intervene and arrest
the lot of them. So ends
the war.

Because there are no hot marksmen on either side,
no one is killed. Well, almost. Early in the fray,
some excited Texan shoots himself in the groin
and takes a while to die.

Justice is never fully served.
Still, most people, after the epic prattle
wanes a little, resume their work
of raising (for those who—right weird
habits, on reflection—eat and wear such ugly, shit-smeared
bawling beasts) cattle.

Wild West Haiku No. 9

The Dalton Gang lays
a flawed plan for Coffeyville:
not one bank but two.

James Earle Fraser, "The End of the Trail," 1915
Plaster, 18 ft. high
(68.01.01) National Cowboy and Western Heritage Museum,
Oklahoma City, OK

James Earle Fraser, *The End of the Trail* (circa 1894)

For Walter Cummins

Still a teen when he modeled this, the sculptor spent
most of his life revising it. His muse returned

time and again to celebrate, lament, repent.
Heaviness, listlessness, loss—here all arcs downward

in defeat. The spear, once raised high to fight or hunt,
slips toward the ground. Both brave and horse droop, dog-tired

from the old struggle against progress; despondent,
they bow in limp submission to the worsting world,

forward wind whipping their backs. But a small extent
of land pedestals them, hooves' purchase unassured.

Carry Nation

1

Though once her father had been prosperous,
he was a wanderer and wound up bust.
She spent her childhood as an invalid,
her thoughts weak and depressing till she turned
to the Good Book. Her first husband, Charles Gloyd,
practiced medicine but never could make
ends meet and drank himself into the grave
after she left. She tried teaching but failed.
Went looking for another mate and found
David Nation, Civil War veteran,
lawyer, editor, Christian minister.
They had few things in common. Scarcely loved
each other. And he viewed with strong distrust
her urge to cleanse humanity. They moved
from place to place but at last settled down,
in 1890, in Medicine Lodge.
And there she got on her high horse about
alcohol, nemesis of many men.
Angel of the jailed, sick, and poor, she closed
the doors of every tavern in the town.

2

Years later she will venture far from home
with iron rod or hatchet to combat
the reign of Demon Rum. And even come
to rail against tobacco, fancy clothes,
Freemasonry, and Britons' taking tea.
And then die penniless, divorced, alone.
Some will praise and commemorate her deeds;
others will raise a glass to her demise.

3

But at this moment she is rolling south,
mind set on her mission in Kiowa.
Buggy full of stones, she has heard God's call.
Her nerves buzz with visions of betterment.
Off to her right stretch hills and buttes and bluffs,
canyons stripped of timber. The savages
have all been killed or civilized. The earth
is red, the air as dry as gypsum. Dry.

Southwestern Kansas, 1897

Land a hundred miles west of Haviland.

A horizontal line, barely curved, cuts
the photograph in two: the lower half
is treeless earth; the upper, cloudless sky.

No railroad tracks. No barn. No horse. No cow.
No chickens. No picnic. No quilting bee.
No school. No dance. No prairie fire. No plague
of locusts. No dust storm. No drought. No hail.
No tornado. No cholera. No debt.
No Indians. Not even loneliness.

Only this: in the center, on that edge,
a tiny spot, rectangular, at first
maybe a blemish in the positive,
then the focus of dismay—someone's house.

McTeague

McTeague . . . Norris described as
the archetypal westerner.

Richard W. Etulain, *Re-imagining the Modern American
West: A Century of Fiction, History, and Art*

A dim-witted buffoon
of a dentist come from
the frontier, lug ill fit
for city life, McTeague,

stressed to the breaking point,
impelled by blood's blind force,
murdered his greedy wife,
stole her money, made off

to Death Valley, and watched,
confused, cuffed to a corpse,
the nothingness that reached
to nowhere, league on league.

Spindletop

The game: a distillate called gasoline.
Damn Standard Oil's skeptical tentacles,
Patillo Higgens, stubborn as a mule,
sticks to his guns. He knows in his guts what
waits, pressured, underneath that hill of sand:
a buried soup of plants and animals,
short lives sea-changed into black gold long since.

And when at last he conjures up his dark
tower, it geysers heavenward, uncapped,
days and nights, barrels raining down to bless
the broad West with wildcatters, roustabouts,
roughnecks, con men, gulls, whores, hoods, gamblers, towns
rising and falling, booms and busts, and all
the myriad going of humankind.

Charles M. Russell, "In Without Knocking," 1909   Oil on canvas, 20⅛" x 29⅞"   (1961.201) Amon Carter Museum, Fort Worth, TX

Charles M. Russell, *In without Knocking* (1909)

Montana sun low, the street bursts
aswirl with horseflesh, gunsmoke, spurs,
hats, dust, stirrups, latigos, reins,
lariats, fenders, poker cards
scattered, one critter fallen, hoof
pushed through the plank walk:

                these are men

with saddles cinched on rough romance,
hellbent for drink, who don't dismount
before they enter a saloon,
men Remington meant when he spoke
of men with the bark on, tough men
whose breed will never quite die out—
Henry Keaton, the Skelton boys,
Matt Price, you, me.

           Give us a wild
ride till we hit the trail at dawn!

Wild West Haiku No. 10

Horses, soldiers, guns,
whiskey, and a Deadwood grave:
Calamity Jane.

Dr. Brewster Higley, the Man Who Wrote "Home on the Range"

Whatever the sweet scenes his rhymes
rehearse, he was married five times
and often undoubtedly heard
many a discouraging word.

Bulgarian-born Modernist Jules Pascin, Who Later Will Hang Himself on the Opening Day of a Major Parisian Exhibition of His Lolita-esque Paintings Indebted to François Boucher and Others, Arrives in New Mexico

He steps off the train,
says the light
is too bright,
and gets back on again.

William S. Hart Harrows Hell's Hinges

For Richard Slotkin

Face and landscape, austere and cactus-lean,
are one, always in movies with the same
predictable nickelodeon plots
plodded through by an actor, Eastern-born,
whose cowboy ways are mostly lies.
                                        Again
the myth unfolds. Blaze Tracey has gone bad,
but he's not rotten to the core, knows right
from wrong. Once his heart is won by a pure
white woman, passion's glances gathering
his will into the Anglo-Saxon church
of manhood, he has to kick ass. Guns drawn,
he bucks Silk Miller and his saloon gang
alone, leaves the scumbag dead, and burns down
the whole town. Blaze and Faith Henley ride off,
headed further west for a better life
out there. Again

                        and again

                                and again.

The Rise and Fall
of Bartholomew "Bat" Masterson

Buffalo hunter, fell gunfighter,
lawman, bar dog, blowhard, sportswriter.

Sarah Winchester

She inherited everything—lock, stock,
and barrel—sick young William Wirt bequeathed.

After she lost her only child, she bought
a modest house in San Jose, became
spiritual, and found a hobbyhorse.

Fortuned indeed, withdrawn in widowhood,
she kept a team of carpenters at work
day and night. Over thirty years they built,
unbuilt, and rebuilt room on room by whim
on whim born of her recluse dream of home.

And when she died, the whole huge hodgepodge sprawled
upon six acres like her own mind's maze,
issue of the hope that doors opening
to drop-off space, secret passages, stairs
stopping at ceilings, halls leading to walls,
windows looking nowhere

               would let her foil
all the souls her family's rifles freed.

Willa Cather

In winter, when Nebraska is shorn bare
and gray as sheet iron, no one
who hasn't grown up there
knows anything
about it; but she did,
though not entirely, since she spent
nine years in Virginia before she left
lush green for little more than soil,
then discovered the truth
under the skin
of its inhabitants.
Their unforgotten stories sparked
lark songs in her, the words she had to sing
to free her life from the heart's cleft
below the cliff of time
crumbling to sky
as mystical as earth,
even when she lived far away.
Through art she lost and gained the thing she long
denied and wanted: waiting, still unpossessed,
the fecund catafalque
of land, the past.

Will Rogers Tells the Story
of Charles M. Russell

The West was in his veins.
Three generations back
his kin had pioneered.
Sixteen, Charley left east
Missouri, hungry for
Montana. Herded sheep
there, but it wouldn't take
as a vocation. Tried
surviving by his wits
in the wilderness. Then
hired on as a nighthawk.

Bored out in big-sky land,
Charley learned how to draw.
On any surface near—
cardboard, birchbark, buckskin.
He did this wonderful
sketch of a famished steer.
Winter of eighty-six.
Barkeep in Utica
with a good eye for art
paid him, maybe in drinks,
to do a piece on wood.

Then Charley lived among
the Bloods a bit and turned
half Indian. Sold more
work, but he had no head
for money. Then met Mame
and hooked up with a girl
with market sense who made
him rich and famous—though
he kept his simple ways.

Older, Charley grew sad.
He said all the best camps
on memory's trail lay
behind him, and he seemed
a stranger in his own
country, lonesome as that
bull skull mounted above
his fireplace. Yet he knew,
even on his deathbed,
the Rocky Mountains still,
in spite of gasoline,
mostly belonged to God.

Wyatt Earp's Last Words

He had a nose for the subjunctive, but his eyes
watched for its opposite. His long
and checkered and ambiguous career
in law and otherwise
stretched to and from a vacant lot
in Arizona, thirty seconds blear
with smoke from shot on shot
resounding in the haze
of year on year
since he was young and strong.

In his declining days,
amid Hollywood's early craze
for Westerns, he forgot
how much of him was fate, how much he chose.

He mumbled at the moment of his close,
"Suppose. . . . Suppose. . . ."

Princess Wenona

Now and again during her many years
performing sure-shot stunts, her name,
like the story of her past, varied some.
Buffalo Bill and Pawnee Bill bestowed this one
when they combined their businesses. She liked it best,
kept it, dressed Indian to match
the billing and to give a sense of what it meant
to be, somehow, Chief Crazy Snake's daughter. She

　　　rode
proud, surrounded by a Wild West
of wood and canvas, popping one by one
the ten glass balls on strings that swung around a pole,
aim unerring even when her horse moved
at full speed. Crowds roared with applause.

Glory abounded.

　　　After Cody's show
folded, she toured with the 101 Ranch.
But then came Western movies, soon
to make her obsolete.
She put on weight and ran through drinks
and husbands one by one.

　　　She ended up
hanging her hat in a cabin on the Salt Fork,
near Ponca City, Oklahoma, an old fake,
solitary save for chickens and stray
dogs, lost in memories of memories,
a creature from another age,
the record-cold dust-bowl winter that would
kill her already darkening the air.

A Poetic History of the American West

81

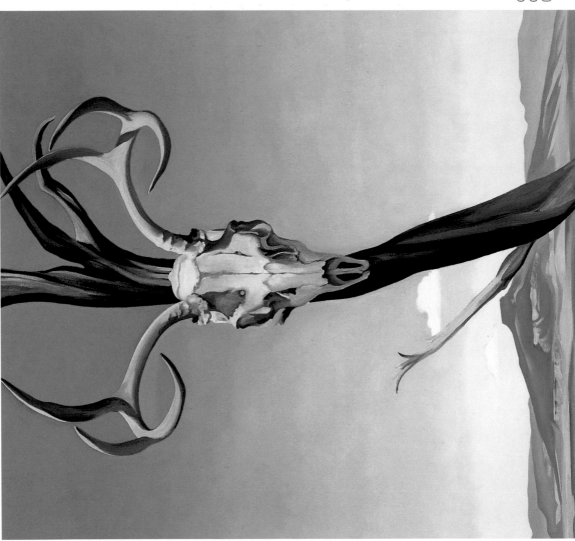

Georgia O'Keeffe, "Deer's Skull with Pedernal," 1936
Oil on canvas, 36" x 30"
(1879) Boston Museum of Fine Arts, Boston, MA,
Georgia O'Keeffe Foundation/Artists Rights
Society, New York, NY

Georgia O'Keeffe, *Deer's Skull with Pedernal* (1936)

Nothing sentimental
about this skull
hung on a twisted branch
to symbolize
the desert it
seems to hover above,
its symmetry
fiercely composed
against clean, distant sky
piercing the eye
sockets with points
of blue—
how much self-portraiture
in such bleached bone?

Zack Miller of the 101 Ranch
Remembers Bill Pickett

That black Choctaw brush buster was half nuts
but a good man, nimble as a gymnast, stout,
loyal, always willin' to have a drink
with friends. No matter what, he did his best.

Bill started out in Texas as a hand
on ranches near Taylor, Georgetown, Round Rock,
then others further south, along the Rio Grande.
Bulldog taught him how to take a cow down
once she's broken free of the hellish dense
overgrowth such animals love to get
themselves ensnarled in. Bill'd leap off his mount,
grab the critter by the horns, dig his heels
into the dirt to bring her to a halt,
sink his teeth in her tender upper lip,
hold on tight till her stubbornness gave out,
and throw her to the ground. Did the same thing,
with more panache, when he was wrestlin' steers
for us on tour. Shortly his private sport
became a part of early rodeo—
though most contestants didn't use their mouths.

After my brothers died and the ranch fell
on hard times, Bill bought a section of land
and tried to make a go of it awhile
but then returned to work for me again
in old age.

      One sunrise when I was sick,
Bill was cuttin' horses in the corral.
A big sorrel reared up and kicked him bad.
The forehooves caught him in the head and chest.
He took eleven painful days to die.

Bill never knew when he was born. I think,
though, he damn sure knew well when he was done.

Roy Rogers

Life was nothing but odd jobs till
he went to Hollywood and changed
his name—a good idea since,
just by the nature of the thing
in the Code of the West, no one
with small eyes in a permanent
smiling squint could ever succeed
anywhere playing Leonard Slye,
King of the Cowboys.

And the rest—

that, as they say, is history.

Slogum House

Gulla's gargantuan greed
controls the show out here on
the Niobrara not quite
a long time ago. She wants
it all, gets it for a while.
She makes thugs of her sons, steals
from settlers, files fraudulent
claims on homesteads till her spread
covers a county, keeps girls
at her roadhouse—the whole schmeer.
But her sins don't satisfy,
and she has to pay the tab
with a slow death and more.   Still,

no one tore off the old mask
of Victorian ideals
of how women were assumed
to act and exposed the dark
nightmare of the female West
the way Mari Sandoz did,
corruption and tragedy
the rule even as she wrote.

Tom Mix

After all those daredevil tricks astride
his wonder horse, daft years in circuses,
five wives, lies about his life as unreal
as reels from his own glitzy movies, big
mansion in Hollywood, ranch here, ranch there,
fancy Western clothes and accouterments,
this hard-ridin', straight-shootin', jovial
boy who came from poverty to love fast
cars and loose women was driving alone
between Tucson and Phoenix when he swerved
to miss construction in the road and sped
onto a washed-out bridge and died quick, neck
snapped—likely, some said, by a suitcase filled
brimful with twenty-dollar coins of gold.

John Steuart Curry

Soon after he finished his finest piece,
a painting on the wall outside
the governor's prim office in the capitol,
the legislature fired him. Those
honorable Kansas lawmakers knew the state
wasn't like that wild-eyed John Brown he'd made,
God's human tornado of vengeance, towering
mad-bearded above flame and blood,
a rifle in his right hand, Bible in his left.
Why paint a radical, a freak,
instead of decent folk? The state wasn't like that
at all. Not at all. Not a bit.

The mural stayed, compelling thought; the artist died
heartbroken five years later on.

Walter Scott

When this Kentucky-born trickster first came
to Death Valley, he was only a kid

who worked on a survey team. The West turned
a key in him. He went on to promote

Bill Cody's show, got notions of his own,
and traveled back—to manufacture gold

fever and prosper on no more than lies,
then rumors bred from lies. Until he hit

the jackpot: a Chicago businessman,
gullible and ill, built him a real dream

castle in the sand. It's there still, a mix
of movie sets where rumors legendize.

Peter Hurd, "The Gate and Beyond," 1952   Egg tempera on panel, 47" x 90"   Permanent Collection, Roswell Museum and Art Center, Roswell, NM   Gift of the Artist   (rmac 1953.7.1)

90

Peter Hurd, *The Gate and Beyond* (1952)

For him, returning to New Mexico
was something as primordial as birth
or death, and here his sense of place is strong,
the scale of the work—almost four feet high,
eight feet long—equal to that of the land.

A ranch. Behind the gaptoothed entry gate,
a hard-packed road and its bordering fence,
five strands of barbwire, recede to the faint
infinity of mountains. To the left
stand a weathered house, corral, windmill, horse
drinking at the tank—the rider no more
than a few brush strokes. Parched earth all about,
plane and sparse, color spare, muted in tone.
The outspread sky: tangible, open, calm.

Jackson Pollock

Whatever gender this
boozehound of a waddy
from Cody, Wyoming,
was, his talent burned out
early in a car crash—
but not before he spilled
and splattered paint enough
to change the rules of art.

When he did his first drip
image, he stood back and
said it reminded him
of his absent father
peeing on a flat rock.

He himself peed a lot
in public settings—out
windows, in flowerpots
and fireplaces, on walls.

"John Wayne"

1

Three-o'clock-in-the-morning courage conjured up
with custom scripts and nostalgic myths, big Duke does,
always, what brave men of the West have gotta do.
A calculated cowboy swagger in his stride,
a punching hitch in his speech, he still walks and talks
the way tall America wants to walk and talk.

2

Marion Morrison, a civvy all his life,
now two decades dead, hated horses, preferred suits
to jeans, and made the Iowa boy in himself
vanish into that phantom icon of last-stand
Manifest Destiny for which Ron Kovic rode
the rank dark bronc of Vietnam and lost his dick.

A Reno Gambler Talks about the Action

You have to play
for a high stake,
out on the edge

where your control
stick starts to shake
and Lady Luck

makes you lose track
of death awhile
better than sex

and a loss can
get you off as
sweet as a win.

That's always been
the national
pastime out west.

The Great Basin

Think rock: ranges of tilted fault blocks rise
in mild slopes on one side, then at the top
drop, on the other, straight
down, down to ground continuing to pull apart.

Think green: bathtub rings on the foothills hint
how filled with life these valleys were
till heat held sway and glaciers waned
and evaporation began.

Think rain: the Sierra Nevada, shadowing
the desert, drinks most clouds dry before they arrive,
leaving barely sufficient wet
for sagebrush, silk grass, cactus, and creosote bush.

Think drainage: what water there is here flows
from a fifth of the West not to the sea
but inland to the termini
of lakes, marshes, salt flats, and sinks.

Think emptiness: a century ago
John Muir said this place was unredeemable
forever, and it still does not contain,
on average, two people per square mile.

Think loneliness: roads seem to stretch
to nowhere and pretty much do,
and even the few cities grow, as if nothing would end,
with folks who don't know who they are.

Think myth: homesteads long left
to the sun's cooking, once
inhabited by bold buckaroo dreams of freedom, haunt
old hearts like cattle skulls.

A Texas Rancher
Speaks of Mesquite

Legume with deep
        wide
roots. Helps the soil.
Real hard wood,
good for fence posts.

Thickets of it so
thick some places you
couldn't get through
to save yer soul.

Probably wind up
downright lost.
Better to stick
to the *senderos*.

Pods full of seeds
rich in sugar food—
for Indians once,
for livestock still.

Leaves ain't much.
Thorny sort of shrub
of a tree though
sometimes they're hefty.

Tried to transplant
one of them things
when I was a kid
and learned you cain't.

You'd have to move
an acre of dirt
with it to git out
all the damn roots.

Margaret Yeager's Ranch

A tumbleweed Eden, her ranch once reached
across a county. Choirs of birds sang there;
deer roamed fearless as pets. Frayed photographs
show her family had held that rugged land
against all comers. Sharing easy smiles,
she told a thousand stories of her life
and laughed when she forgot the times and names.
There was nothing she had not learned to love.

But now, too old, she's gone. Bulldozers drown
the scent of life that lingers, scrape the land
to build a landing strip for grander dreams.
Run-down, empty, her house is left to fall.
At noon the ancient wind blows long warm sighs,
soft laughter, through the windows' broken smiles.

Eastwood Western

Need for revenge swells
like frustrated sex.

Long extreme close-ups
of men's faces drawn
and red from the sun.
A guitar churns on.

Interminable.

A hard, white wait. White
as the whites of eyes.
Then hands go for guns.

Loud as howitzers.

The stranger without
a name grits his teeth.
Chews his cigar. Rides
into dense heat waves.

Unrelenting dust.

Homage to Philip Marlowe

You are the tough-guy gumshoe in the lost
heart of every hard-boiled American male,
who cannot be, ever, anyone else
but Natty Bumppo in the wilderness
of overcivilized Los Angeles.
There is only one American tale.

The streets are a kind of quicksand, surreal,
where you defend the same world you resist.
You want it to be safe and yet not dull.
Anachronous, skillful, you must distrust
everyone, even Chingachgook himself.
The contradictions will not be resolved.

Where you move, each violent crime connects
vaguely to others your own presence seems
to breed. You are alone. Logic does not
pertain in murderous America out
anywhere at all on the steel frontier
that started its big sleep so long ago.

And you are seldom completely untouched,
though women, in the last analysis,
are dangerous, trapping. They make you sick.
But it is hope that drives you, not despair,
as you drive through the photoactive haze
of daybreak after another tense night.

You take your share but never stay. You bite
the handkerchief, jump, and run, like Huck Finn,
for the territory's uncertain edge.
In the end the motives are still not clear.
Little is solved, and there is no appeal.
Even the authorities are paid off.

Reality is a snarl of dark threads
leading nowhere finally or too far,
and even your creator does not know
or guess how many passions are in play,
dizzying accidents, complexities
of the corrupt. Chinatown. Chinatown.

Donald Worster

Arid plain behind him, he sits upon the shore
along a concrete-lined canal
in Kern County, California. While he watches a stream
that's not a stream, by which no willows grow
and no herons or blackbirds nest,
he ponders historical images to warn the West
to set its lands in order after so much fierce
avarice for water. He chooses one. Remembering
how, from the time of Mesopotamia on,
all great hydraulic empires fell
into the infrastructure trap
and built more monumental irrigation works
till ecological backlash caught up,
he visions Mongol horsemen as they storm
athwart the deserted devastation of what was once
fertile fields and the lush gardens of Babylon
and find ditches choked with silt and soil white
with alkalinity. Thus he foresees for us
regional self-destruction, however long
evadable, as inevitable
through the remaking of nature to fit ourselves,
by this bleak parable of unpredictable
but sure predicament, mistakenly unmade.

Richard Brautigan Found Dead

You ran out of something, one
of those things you wrote about
in your easy, compressed way.

I always thought darkness lurked
in you, beneath that gentle pose:
you drank by the case, got into guns.

After you shot yourself, your body lay
leaking through that old house
in Bolinas for a month.

They're going to have to check
the dental records. A friend said
you died of American loneliness.

You could have written that.
Hardly anyone I know now knows
or remembers who you were.

Family Members Shot to Death:
A Pathetic Western

Under that head on page ten
of the daily *Capital*:
another story of no
evidence that anyone
did this other than the man
of the house, apparently
unemployed (something police
are checking out), but no real
word on how an average poke
who started out with a smile
and the bootshine of his hope
got into such hidden deep
trouble, whole novels of grief,
a curt column on page ten.

The True Patriot: An Epitaph for Edward Abbey

On one imperative he stayed intent:
to save his country from its government.

The Marlboro Man

Raw life his own,
he who would ride,
hard-eyed, alone,
the high West wide
for a smoke died.

The Lone Ranger, 1991

Chauffeured in a limo or rolled about
in his wheelchair, he still wears
that famous getup but has grown
crabby. He hangs out from time to time
at the Cowboy Hall of Fame to prime
new members and—hellfire, doubt
it not, you post-frontier killers—
insists on being called Lone.

Wild Rogue Rodeo,
Central Point, Oregon, 1991

Belly low, then
bowed in the air,
now swift, now slow,
the animal
spins left, left, left,
well a whirlpool
of hide and horn.

Wade Leslie, yet
unknown, maintains
control, shows sharp
style, and becomes
the first to earn
a perfect score.

Never a bull
like Wolfman Skoal.

Fred DuBray, President of the Inter-tribal Bison Cooperative, Tells His Story of the West

When a storm rams
across the plains,

buffalo stand
and face the wind;

but cattle turn
their backs and run.

Chris McCandless

Another innocent idealist, he gave away
his earthly goods and wandered off
the reservation of suburbia
into the outback of Alaska, geared with just
a small-bore rifle and a bag of rice,
to search for someplace blank.

Months later, isolate
at his adventure's end, he starved
in an abandoned school bus, mind at last
as mapless as the West he wished.

On the Rez

In Dulce, New Mexico, through the dust
along Jicarilla Boulevard in front

of a ramshackle liquor store, an old
Apache walks by, stooped and slow

under the midsummer sun. In tow:
two dogs, also stooped and slow.

Wolf in a Western Zoo

Is this Fenris, the monstrous wolf, who will
break free at the world's end
and eat the sun?

Haven't we had enough of ignorant
hatred of wolves, enough
of killing wolves

until we've nearly wiped the wilderness
clean of wolves, of the wild
wolves represent,

shy animals with their own lives to live
made some image inside
ourselves we fear?

The Day William Stafford Died

You never wanted a memorial.
Likewise, none of that Callimachus-weeping-over-
    Heraclitus crap
for me, Bill. I worked the news
out of my system as soon as it arrived.
Took it like a man. Had some drinks.
Inspected the lawn, my sun-baked world
Autumn was already hauling off to hell
in her hand basket. Rolled out
the mower and said to myself what you always said
about writing: just start the thing
going, take it a step at a time, and see
where you wind up.

And here I am, sweating in the shade
after the solar satori of alcohol.

You went so far west, mile after mile
of mile after mile, that you wound up
a cosmic citizen. And where
are you now? Probably
you're tinkering together a poem about the place.

This morning the sun came out from behind
a rock and followed your heart that had room
for anything, even the ordinary wonder of death.

I have a picture of you in my head:
confident, gentle, comfortable
in one of your worn sweaters, keen eyes
holding their steady gaze.

But there is more. How can I get it into words?
You have always been
my Roy Rogers, king
of the cowboy Buddhas in the prairie schooner of Ra.

In your modest, powerful way
you continue to teach,
a lesson in every line.

It has been a long day, Bill.
Wherever I look is your soul.

An Inhabitant of the San Luis Valley
Ventilates Himself on the Matter of Bizarre
Animal Mutilations in the Region

Most involve cattle. But the case that first
had real attention zooming down on us,
now almost thirty years ago, concerned
an Appaloosa mare Nellie and Burl
Lewis boarded at the King place a few
miles south of the Great Sand Dunes. She was stripped
of flesh from the neck up and drained of blood,
chest organs somehow surgically removed
by heat, with all the cuts laser-precise.
A medicinal smell, incense-like, hung
over the area. Bushes blown flat.
Strange holes poked in the ground. Burn and scorch
     marks

scattered around the meadow. Curious
as hell too was how dead-run hoofprints stopped
a hundred feet from where the carcass lay.
Sometime the night before, Henry King's mom
thought she'd seen a large object pass above
the ranch house. Others saw lights bob and weave
throughout the valley. Field day for the press.

Since then dozens of cattle have been found—
no signs of struggle, the rectum cored out,
sex organs extracted neat as could be,
udders and teats nicely excised. An eye
gone as well maybe, an ear, or the heart.

Who does this? Aliens? For what reason? "Why,"
a neighbor woman asked, "would anyone
cross millions of miles in a UFO
just to castrate our little Beauregard?"
It makes no damn sense to beam up a cow—
unless, of course, you direly *need* those parts.
Is the Air Force implicated? A lot
of folks have witnessed helicopter flights
that correlate—up to a point. The more
you investigate, the weirder it gets.
Meditators, channelers, satanists,
psychics, astrologers, Taos-hum freaks,
New Agers wanting to build pyramids—
God knows who knows what about what's out there.

As for me, I just keep an open mind,
stay on the Internet, and wait for new
instructions from Zeta Reticulae.

Bigfoot

Salish bandersnatch,
hairy leviathan,
fugitive phantom
of wilderness, Sasquatch
walks all the way from
western Washington
east to the Wasatch
Mountains, then on
up to Saskatchewan,
and back—unwatched
by anyone.

Over Coffee (Not Unleaded) at the Cassoday Cafe, a Veteran of the Range Puts the Recent Vogue of Buckaroo Chic into Historical Perspective

All these New
Western turds—
tolerance
wears down thin.

Hell, I rode
drag back when
cowboy was
still two words.

Simpson Agonistes

Helicopter voyeurs, all of us watched
the white Ford Bronco in that sluggish chase
down Los Angeles freeways to nowhere
but home.

   We watched from telephoto height
the same vehicle in his driveway, stopped
at last, abstract as an Iraqi tank
that might explode in the video game
of death.

   We watched even when the screen turned
into night—tube-numbed eyes still hungry for
something out of myth—and the only stripe
of god on earth, a man lost in love's old
tragedy, our hero of holy sport,
Othello-like, took the gun from his head,
stepped into the dark, and gave himself up
not to the Furies of an absolute
justice but to the profiteers of law
and the ringmasters of celebrity.

M. T. Liggett of Mullinville, Kansas, Expounds on His Totem-Pole Art

I'm a retired military man, don't
buy shit from politicians. All that work
in the field along Highway 54
shows you the truth. From the district school board
to the White House, no one escapes the wrath
of my trusty Pro-Cut electric torch.

If what I do offends somebody, great.
That's why I put it there. One thing about
art—it's infinite. You'll never run out
of subjects 'cause these political types—
Democrats and Republicans, there's not
a plugged nickel's worth of difference, you know—
they're always screwing up. And when a thought
hits, you've got to stop what you're at and cut
that thought before it's lost. Cut it to last—
in iron. Paint it bright. See that windmill
of words topped by a "Feminazi" sign?
That's for Hillary. Those guys with their heads
stuck in a toilet—well, they're *local* fools.
For Janet Reno, there's my Auschwitz piece.

Most people I know are automatons.
God help them. What a waste. A junkyard dog
learns faster than they do. You can't excel
unless you rebel, and I'm a whole-hog
dissenter, not your average, everyday,
run-of-the-mill intelligentsia.

People fear me. Hell, I'm the most disliked
person in Kiowa County, hands down.

I'm going to do these things till I die,
and then I'll get some mortician to fix
my fingers in a fist, middle one raised.

A Farmwife Tells about
Tornados in Kansas

The last time
one blew through

here and came
way too close,

something in
my old man

snapped like a
pot-metal

hex wrench. Damn
funnel tore

the tires right
off his new

tractor, and
he's not come

up from the
basement since.

The Last Best Place, 1997

This full moon over
Missoula, Montana, glows
like a campfire after
the hands have opened their rolls
and bedded down forever.

Ted Binion

His father, Benny Binion, was as well
father of the Horseshoe, a character
from Vegas' high-limit heyday who wore
Western-style suits and shirts with solid gold
buttons, detested neckties, and could size
you up and hew you down with the quick flint
flash of his eyes. He lived the golden rule:
because he had the gold, he made the rules.
Business was good and stayed good till he died.

But Ted got into shit above his head,
a weirder West than Benny ever knew.
After drugs cost his license for the club,
a topless-dancer girlfriend claimed she found
his corpse draped with a comforter, boots off,
muted game show flickering in the dark,
empty bottle of anxiety pills
fallen on the floor. Next night, police caught
three men in a nearby town digging up
a truckload hoard of silver bars and such.
Suspicions lasted way beyond the strange
funeral, at which an impeached judge gave
the eulogy before a coffin decked
with cowboy gear and the Doors sang "The End."

Epitaph of a Lonely Rancher

I still hope some
cowgirl will come
wanting a ride,
to saddle me
and straddle me
and peel my pride.

The Interior West

When the low sun
dims to maroon,
this wilderness,
as dry as lime
from precipice
to slope to plain,
summons deep fear:
lorn as a moon
lit by a star
far from our own,
it speaks to us
of the long time
before we came
and the long time
after we're gone.

Edd Hayes, "The Champ," 1988
Bronze, larger than life-size, at the entrance
of the ProRodeo Hall of Fame and
Museum of the American Cowboy,
Colorado Springs, CO

The Champ: Casey Tibbs
before the ProRodeo Hall of Fame

Danger and awe and challenge
all in one frozen plunge
beneath a snow-still mountain:
wild pastoral in bronze.

The West's eternal emblem,
its dialectic game:
a bronco yet unbroken,
a rider never tame.

Sources

What follows hardly accounts for the origins and final forms of the preceding poems, which are indebted to more experiences than I can mention without etherizing the reader. It's simply an alphabetical list of published sources upon which I've variously depended in writing many of those poems. Some provided factual information. Some shook up my assumptions and helped me see afresh. Some harbored seeds from which poetic flowers grew. Some hinted at a voice to be developed. Some included prose text that—with selection, lineation, and other shaping—became more or less found poetry. Some harbored useful citations from yet other sources. Raw material for the imagination's work may have slipped from some into the Western gallimaufry of my mind unconsciously—for which action of the muse I'm most grateful. At any rate, historiography, in this case mostly in the form of representative and frequently revisionary life-writings of one kind or another (portraits, ecphrases, vignettes, monologues, brief narratives, epitaphic synopses, and so on—with no pretension to comprehensiveness), requires sources; here, in as thorough a catalogue as I can compile, are mine.

Abbey, Edward. *One Life at a Time, Please.* New York: Henry Holt, 1988.

Ambrose, Stephen E. *Undaunted Courage: Meriwether Lewis, Thomas Jefferson, and the Opening of the American West.* New York: Simon and Schuster, 1996.

Aquila, Richard, ed. *Wanted Dead or Alive: The American West in Popular Culture.* Urbana: University of Illinois Press, 1996.

Armitage, Susan, and Elizabeth Jameson, eds. *The Women's West.* Norman: University of Oklahoma Press, 1987.

Arnason, H. H. *History of Modern Art: Painting, Sculpture, Architecture.* 2d ed., rev. Englewood Cliffs, NJ: Prentice-Hall; New York: Abrams, 1977.

Bennett, Charles. "Exploits of Elfego Baca." *Santa Fean,* January–February 1994, pp. 14–16.

Bierds, Linda. "Light, Steam." In *Heart and Perimeter,* pp. 39–40. New York: Henry Holt, 1991.

Blevins, Winfred. *Dictionary of the American West.* New York: Facts on File, 1993.

Broder, Patricia Janis. *The American West: The Modern Vision*. Boston: Little, Brown, New York Graphic Society Books, 1984.

Brown, Dee. *Wondrous Times on the Frontier*. New York: HarperCollins, 1991.

Carpenter, Kelley S. "The Art of Politics." *Lawrence Journal-World*, 21 April 1996, p. 1D.

Cather, Willa. *My Ántonia*. 1918. Reprint. Boston: Houghton Mifflin, 1988.

—. *The Professor's House*. 1925. Reprint. New York: Random House, Vintage Books, 1973.

—. *The Song of the Lark*. 1915. Reprint. Boston: Houghton Mifflin, 1988.

Chamberlain, Samuel E. *My Confession*. 1956. Reprint. Lincoln: University of Nebraska Press, 1987.

Christensen, Jon. "The Great Basin: America's Wasteland Seeks a New Identity." *High Country News*, 3 April 1995, pp. 1, 8–9.

Cirlot, J. E. *A Dictionary of Symbols*, trans. Jack Sage. New York: Philosophical Library, 1962.

Crichton, Kyle S. *Law and Order, Ltd.: The Rousing Life of Elfego Baca of New Mexico*. Santa Fe: New Mexican Publishing Corporation, 1928.

Dary, David. *Cowboy Culture: A Saga of Five Centuries*. Lawrence: University Press of Kansas, 1989.

Editors of Time-Life Books. *The Trailblazers*. New York: Time-Life Books, 1973.

—. *The Wild West*. N.p.: Warner Books, 1993.

Eliot, T. S. *The Waste Land*. In *The Complete Poems and Plays, 1909–1950*, pp. 37–55. New York: Harcourt, Brace and World, 1962.

Ellmann, Richard. *Oscar Wilde*. New York: Knopf, 1988.

Etulain, Richard W. *Re-Imagining the Modern American West: A Century of Fiction, History, and Art*. Tucson: University of Arizona Press, 1996.

Goetzmann, William H., and William N. Goetzmann. *The West of the Imagination*. New York: Norton, 1986.

Gould, Lewis L. "A. S. Mercer and the Johnson County War: A Reappraisal." *Arizona and the West: A Quarterly Journal of History* 7 (1965): 5–20.

Gragg, Rod. *The Old West Quiz and Fact Book*. 1986. Reprint. New York: Promontory Press, 1993.

Hansen, Ron. *The Assassination of Jesse James by the Coward Robert Ford*. New York: Norton, 1983.

Hoy, Jim. *Cowboys and Kansas: Stories from the Tallgrass Prairie*. Norman: University of Oklahoma Press, 1995.

Hufsmith, George W. *The Wyoming Lynching of Cattle Kate, 1889*. Glendo, WY: High Plains Press, 1993.

Jennings, Kate F. *Remington and Russell and the Art of the American West*. New York: Smithmark, 1993.

Kelley, Matt. "Indians Work to Restore Buffalo Herds on Tribal Lands." *Lawrence Journal-World*, 17 January 1993, p. 3C.

Krakauer, Jon. *Into the Wild*. New York: Villard, 1996.

Limerick, Patricia Nelson. *The Legacy of Conquest: The Unbroken Past of the American West*. New York: Norton, 1987.

Lindsay, Merrill. *One Hundred Great Guns: An Illustrated History of Firearms*. New York: Walker, 1967.

McCord, Hugh. "Meriwether Lewis: Murder or Suicide?" *Louis L'Amour Western Magazine* 1, no. 1 (1993): 97–103.

McCoy, Max. *The Sixth Rider: A Novel of the Dalton Gang*. New York: Doubleday, 1991.

McGinnis, Bruce. *Reflections in Dark Glass: The Life and Times of John Wesley Hardin*. Denton: University of North Texas Press, 1996.

McMurtry, Larry. *Buffalo Girls: A Novel*. New York: Simon and Schuster, 1990.

McNeal, T. A. *When Kansas Was Young*. New York: Macmillan, 1922.

Martin, Gene, and Mary Martin. *Trail Dust: A Quick Picture History of the Santa Fe Trail*. Manitou Springs, CO: Martin Associates, 1972.

Mercer, Asa Shinn. *The Banditti of the Plains; or, The Cattlemen's Invasion of Wyoming in 1892, the Crowning Infamy of the Ages*. 1894. Reprint. Norman: University of Oklahoma Press, 1954.

Momaday, N. Scott. *In the Presence of the Sun: Stories and Poems*. New York: St. Martin's Press, 1992.

Norris, Frank. *McTeague: A Story of San Francisco*. 1899. Reprint. New York: Viking Penguin, 1982.

Perkins, David. "Heart of Weirdness: Myth and Mystery in the San Luis Valley." *Spirit: The Magazine of the Rocky Mountain Southwest*, Fall–Winter 1994–95, pp. 20–25.

Phillips, Charles, and Alan Axelrod, eds. *Encyclopedia of the American West*. 4 vols. New York: Simon and Schuster Macmillan, 1996.

Pyle, Robert Michael. *Where Bigfoot Walks: Crossing the Dark Divide*. Boston: Houghton Mifflin, 1995.

Riley, Glenda. "Mari Sandoz's *Slogum House*: Greed as Woman." *Great Plains Quarterly* 16 (1996): 29–41.

Rohrbough, Malcolm J. *Days of Gold: The California Gold Rush and the American Nation*. Berkeley and Los Angeles: University of California Press, 1997.

Rosa, Joseph G. *Wild Bill Hickok: The Man and His Myth*. Lawrence: University Press of Kansas, 1996.

Sandoz, Mari. *Slogum House*. 1937. Reprint. New York: Avon Books, 1968.

Schlissel, Lillian, Vicki L. Ruiz, and Janice Monk, eds. *Western Women: Their Land, Their Lives*. Albuquerque: University of New Mexico Press, 1988.

Shirley, Glenn. *Red Yesterdays*. Wichita Falls, TX: Nortex Press, 1977.

Slatta, Richard W. *Cowboys of the Americas*. New Haven: Yale University Press, 1990.

Slotkin, Richard. *Gunfighter Nation: The Myth of the Frontier in Twentieth-Century America*. New York: Atheneum, 1992.

Smith, Helena Huntington. *The War on Powder River: The History of an Insurrection*. Lincoln: University of Nebraska Press, 1966.

Stegner, Wallace. *Where the Bluebird Sings to the Lemonade Springs: Living and Writing in the West*. New York: Random House, 1992.

Stern, Jane, and Michael Stern. *Way Out West*. New York: HarperCollins, 1993.

Thomson, David. *Silver Light*. New York: Knopf, 1990.

Truettner, William H., ed. *The West as America: Reinterpreting Images of the Frontier, 1820–1920*. Washington: Smithsonian Institution Press, 1991.

Weber, David J. *The Spanish Frontier in North America*. New Haven: Yale University Press, 1992.

West, Naida. *River of Red Gold*. Rancho Murieta, CA: Bridge House Books, 1996.

Westbrook, Max. Afterword to *The Virginian: A Horseman of the Plains*, by Owen Wister. New York: NAL Penguin, Signet Classic, 1979.

White, Richard. *"It's Your Misfortune and None of My Own": A New History of the American West*. Norman: University of Oklahoma Press, 1991.

Williamson, Harold F. *Winchester: The Gun That Won the West*. Washington: Combat Forces Press, 1952.

Wills, Garry. *John Wayne's America: The Politics of Celebrity*. New York: Simon and Schuster, 1997.

Wister, Owen. *The Virginian: A Horseman of the Plains*. 1902. Reprint. New York: NAL Penguin, Signet Classic, 1979.

Wooden, Wayne S., and Gavin Ehringer. *Rodeo in America: Wranglers, Roughstock, and Paydirt*. Lawrence: University Press of Kansas, 1996.

Worster, Donald. *Under Western Skies: Nature and History in the American West*. New York: Oxford University Press, 1992.

Yost, Nellie Snyder. *Buffalo Bill: His Family, Friends, Failures, and Fortunes*. Chicago: Swallow, 1979.

—. *Medicine Lodge: The Story of a Kansas Frontier Town*. Chicago: Swallow, 1970.